FIELD TRIPS

The Fire Station

Stuart A. Kallen
ABDO & Daughters

Published by Abdo & Daughters, 4940 Viking Drive, Suite 622, Edina, Minnesota 55435.

Printed in the United States.

Cover and Interior Photo credits: Peter Arnold, Inc.
Superstock
Illustration: Ben Dann Lander
Edited by Julie Berg

Library of Congress Cataloging-In-Publication Data

Kallen, Stuart A., 1955-
The fire station / Stuart A. Kallen.
p. cm. — (Field trips)
Includes Index.
Summary: Briefly describes what goes on at a fire station and the work of fire fighters.
ISBN 1-56239-710-9
1. Fire stations—Juvenile literature. [1. Fire departments. 2. Fire fighters.] I. Title. II. Series.
TH9148.K35 1997
628.9'2—dc20   96-22579
                                                                          CIP
                                                                          AC

Contents

Fire! Fire!

When the fire bell rings, fire fighters have to put on their **gear**. They put on rubber coats and hats. They put on air tanks so they can breathe when they are in smoke-filled buildings. They put on rubber boots to keep their feet dry.

Fire fighters have special places where they ride on the truck. Some drive. Others ride on the back, holding onto handles. A long **hook-and-ladder** has an extra fire fighter steering from the back.

**Opposite page: Fire fighters' gear
hung up and ready for action!**

The Fire Station

You'll see all the tools used by fire fighters when you visit a fire station. When you walk up to the station it looks like a giant garage. That's where the shiny, red fire trucks are kept. There's an apartment attached to the garage. That's where the fire fighters live. Maybe the fire dog will come out to greet you.

There's a radio room where calls for help come in. Fire equipment is stored carefully and kept in top shape. Fire fighters check tools and trucks every day. They clean water hoses. They sharpen axes. When the fire alarm rings, fire fighters must know that their tools will work.

Fires start without warning, so there must be fire fighters on duty at all times at the fire station. They cook their meals in a kitchen. They sleep in bunks. And when a fire starts, they slide down brass poles to the fire truck garage.

People who don't live in large cities are sometimes protected by **volunteer** fire fighters. Volunteers are people with other jobs who agree to fight fires whenever they start, day or night. Volunteer fire departments still have their own fire stations.

Fire fighters have to keep their equipment in good shape.

The Fire Fighter's Job

Fire fighters are men and women who risk their lives every day. Their most important job is to put out fires that threaten lives and **property**. They must learn how to do this at fire fighters' school.

Fire fighters drive those long red fire trucks to help pump the water onto fires. All those huge hoses shoot water onto fires. You'll see ladders that fire fighters use to climb into the windows of burning buildings. They use the axes to break through burning doors and walls.

Fire fighters also rescue people who have been in car accidents. They use a tool called the "**jaws of life**" to pry crushed car metal. This allows people to escape from a wreck.

Fire fighters will be called to help rescue people from rivers and lakes. They save people who are drowning. They put out fires on burning boats.

Fire fighters are heroes who save hundreds of people's lives every day.

**Fire fighting
is a risky job.**

Between Fires

When there are no emergencies, fire fighters can relax. Their equipment is hung and always ready. Sometimes they play basketball. Sometimes they exercise. Maybe they just want to read a book or take a nap. Fire fighters keep their trucks clean and ready for emergencies.

But when the fire bell rings, the fire fighters stop whatever they're doing and spring into action.

Opposite page: When fire fighters are not putting out fires they relax and do normal things. But when the fire bell rings, they are always ready to go.

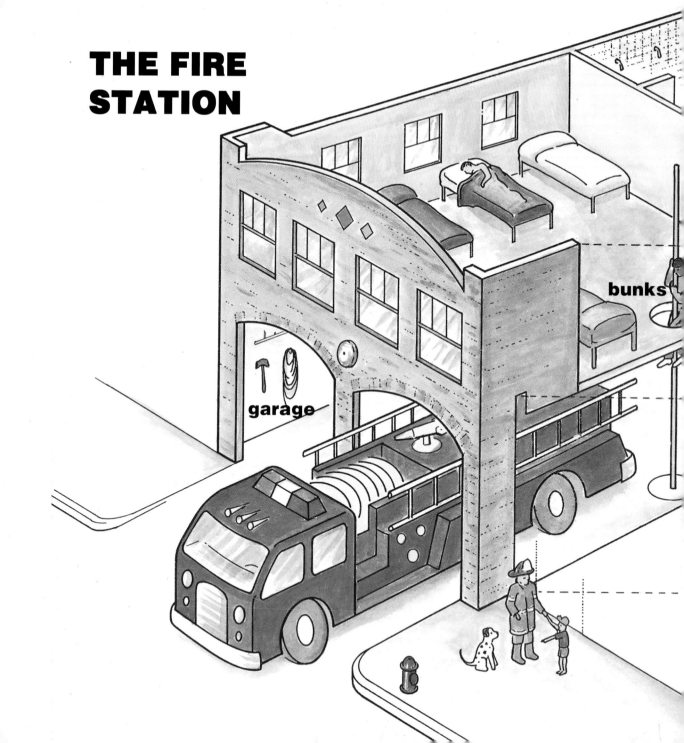

THE FIRE STATION

bunks

garage

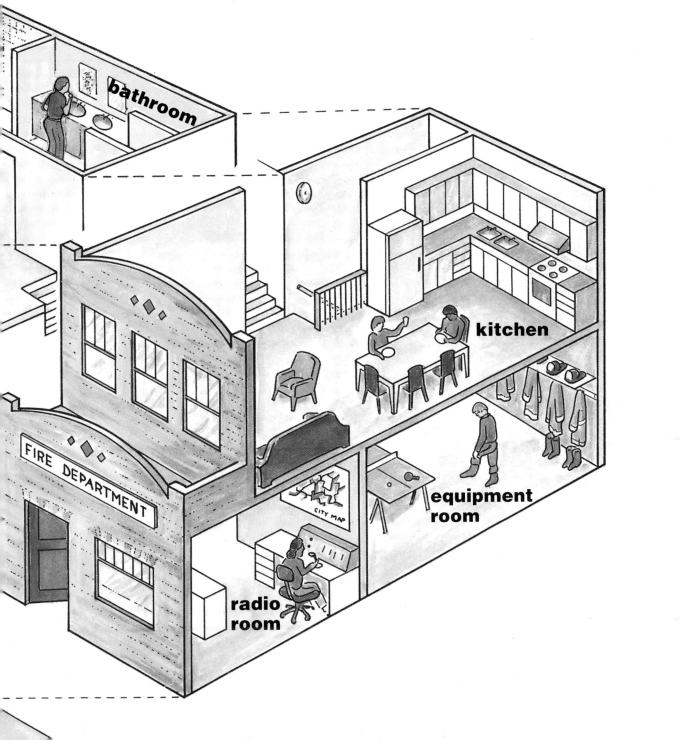

bathroom

kitchen

FIRE DEPARTMENT

equipment room

radio room

CITY MAP

Fire Trucks

The giant doors on a fire station open up to let fire trucks in and out. The garage where the fire engines are parked is always clean and dry. If the fire alarm sounds, fire fighters know that their fire engine will be warmed up and ready to go. You might see fire fighters working on the fire engines. They check the oil, fill them up with gas, and keep the tires full of air.

The long fire trucks are called **hook-and-ladders**. Their long ladders are used to rescue people in tall buildings. Fire trucks with long hoses are **pumpers**. They pump water far distances like a huge squirt gun.

Opposite page: Fire fighters check their engines regularly.

Putting Out a Fire

When fire fighters arrive at the scene of a fire, they go into action. Each fire fighter has a special job. The **fire chief** directs the fire fight, and makes sure that the fire gets put out.

Some fire fighters break holes in the windows and roof of a burning building. This lets out smoke and flames and makes it easier to rescue people inside.

Other fire fighters attach hoses to **fire hydrants** and **pumper** trucks. They aim streams of water at the flames. Some fire fighters run inside the building with hoses to put out fires inside.

Once the fire is out, fire fighters must go inside the building to make sure every last spark is out. Then the tired fire fighters must roll up their hoses, pack up their equipment, and take it back to the fire station. There it is cleaned and repaired for the next fire.

Opposite page: Fire fighters putting out a house fire.

Brave Fire Fighters

Fighting fires is hard, dangerous work. Sometimes fire fighters lose their lives in fires. Almost every city and town has a monument to fire fighters. Some are honored with medals and decorations.

Fire fighters don't just rescue people. They rescue dogs, cats, and other pets.

You can be sure that if there is an emergency a fire fighter will be there as soon as possible.

Opposite page: Fire fighters have to be brave when trying to control dangerous fires.

19

Visit a Fire Station

Kids love the shiny red fire engines. And fire fighters love kids. You can go to a nearby fire station to say hello. The fire fighters will be glad to see you. As long as there's no emergency, fire fighters will be happy to give you a tour of their station.

You can climb on the trucks. You can see where the equipment is kept. You might even get to slide down the fire pole!

But if the fire alarm goes off, get out of the way! The fire fighters will be gone in a flash.

Opposite page: Fire fighters are friendly and always ready to help.

Glossary

fire chief - highest ranking officer in the fire department.

fire hydrant - a pipe with a valve from which water may be drawn.

gear - equipment designed for some specific purpose.

hook-and-ladder - a fire engine equipped with a long ladder and hooked poles for rescuing people.

jaws of life - a tool used for cutting metal in wrecked cars to free trapped victims.

property - something owned, such as a house or a car.

pumper - a machine or device that moves or forces water out of itself.

volunteer - a person who performs a service without being paid.

Index